RESET

A 7-Day Devotional
for Restoring Your Connection
with God

*Find Peace, Clarity, and Strength as You
Realign Your Heart With Him*

by

D.D. Stumpf

EverLove Press

Some material in this devotional is adapted from the author's earlier work The Love of God: Your Guide to Supernatural Intelligence.

Published by EverLove Press

ISBN: 979-8-9931497-2-1

Cover design by G.M. Stumpf

Printed in the United States of America

For permissions, inquiries, or correspondence: contact@everlovepress.com

Table of Contents

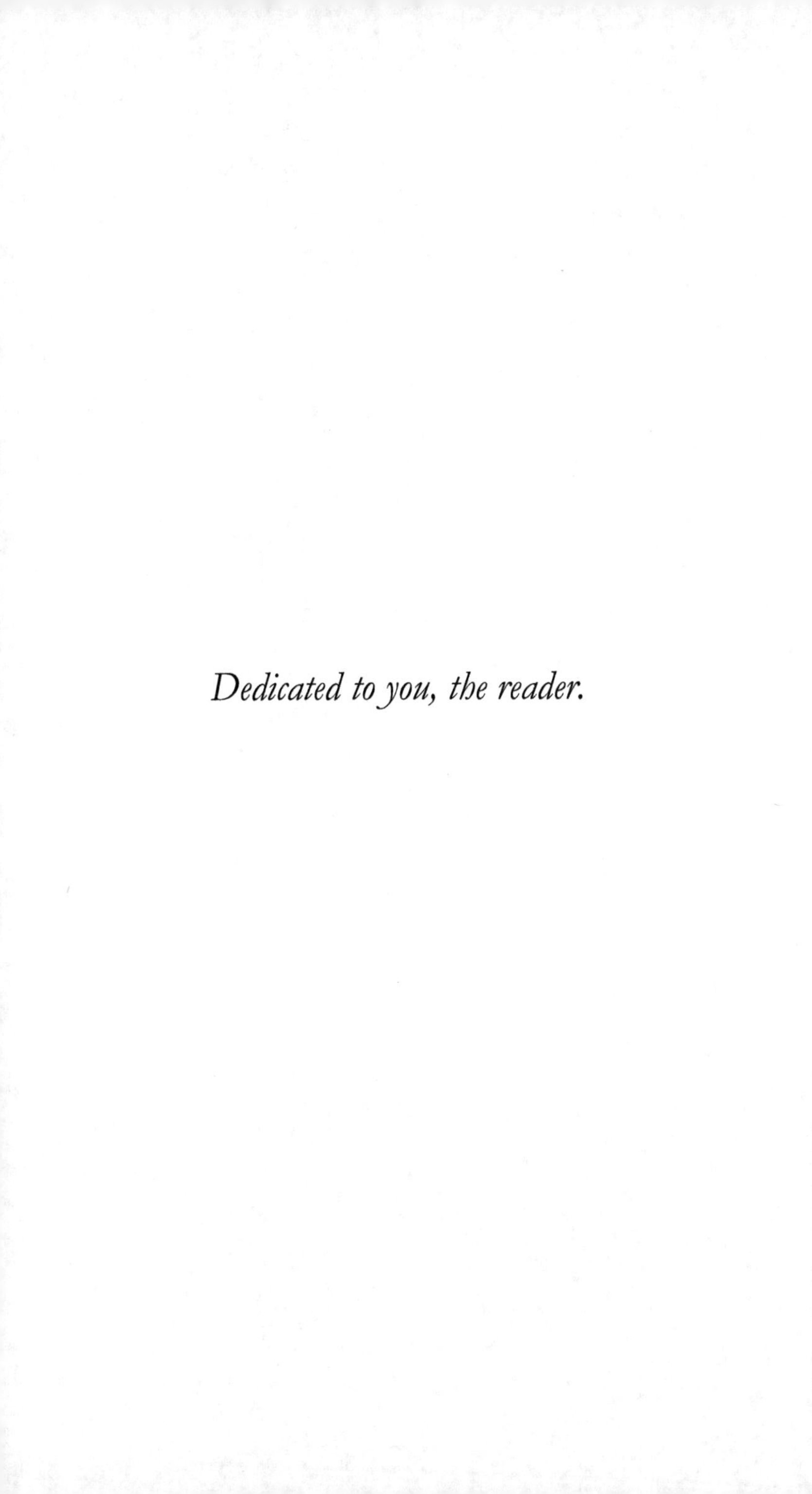

Dedicated to you, the reader.

Introduction

Life can move at a pace our hearts were never meant to carry. Responsibilities press in. Distractions tug at our attention. And before we realize it, the nearness we once felt with God begins to fade into the background.

RESET was created for moments like these.

It's an invitation to slow down, breathe deeply, and return your heart to the One who loves you most. These pages are here to help you pause, refocus, and realign your soul with Him.

You'll notice the author's voice is intentionally gentle and minimal throughout this devotional. That is by design.

Each page is meant to guide you quietly into a personal moment with God—where you open your heart before Him, and He meets you with His presence, His comfort, and His wisdom.

RESET is a seven day journey for seasons when you need to draw close to God again— quickly, simply, and deeply.

Each day offers a single truth from Scripture to anchor your heart. You'll read one entry per day for seven days. When you reach the end, begin again at Day 1.

This rhythm is intentional.

Repeating these seven days allows God's truth to move from something you know to something you live.

Returning to the same Scriptures and reflections gives them space to settle into your heart, shaping your thoughts, your decisions, and your inner life.

Reading each day's devotional is just the beginning; transformation unfolds as you let its truth shape your day.

Let each day's message stay with you—something you carry, ponder, and return to throughout the day.

As you meditate on it, God will meet you in quiet moments, unexpected places, and ordinary tasks, gently drawing your heart back to Him again and again.

This is why repetition matters.

Cognitive research tells us that revisiting the same truths strengthens the pathways in our minds, making them easier to remember and live out.

But long before science discovered this, Scripture taught it. God often invites His people to "remember," "meditate," and "keep these words before you."

Repetition isn't redundancy—it's formation.

Think of it like planting seeds.

Reading something once scatters seeds on the surface. Reading it again presses those seeds deeper into the soil of your heart, where they can take root, grow strong, and bear fruit.

RESET is your invitation to a fresh start—something you can return to whenever life feels scattered.

These seven days are designed to help you find peace, clarity, and strength as you realign your heart with God, day after day.

Come to me, all you who are weary and burdened, and I will give you rest.

— Matthew 11:28 (NIV)

How to Use RESET

RESET is designed to be simple, peaceful, and deeply personal. These seven days are first and foremost a space for you and God.

If at any point you feel led to invite someone into the journey, consider walking through it together—reflecting, encouraging, and growing side by side.

1. Read one entry each day.
2. Carry the day's truth with you.
3. Repeat the seven-day cycle.

WELCOME TO YOUR RESET

Day 1 —
Reset Your Mind

Scripture

"Be transformed by the renewing of your mind." — Romans 12:2

Reflection

A reset begins in your thoughts. Before anything changes around you, something shifts within you.

Today is about clearing mental clutter and making space for God's truth again.

Heart Moment

Let go of the thoughts that drain you.

Hold onto the ones that strengthen you.

Prayer

Dear God, renew my mind today. Replace old patterns with Your truth. Amen.

Takeaway

A reset starts with a thought.

Pause here.

You've finished Day 1.

"Be transformed by the renewing of your mind."
— Romans 12:2

Return tomorrow for Day 2.

Day 2 —
Reset Your Peace

Scripture

"My peace I give you." — *John 14:27*

Reflection

Peace isn't found in perfect circumstances — it's found in God's presence.

Today is about releasing the tension you've been carrying and letting God settle your spirit.

Heart Moment

Breathe deeply.

Let peace rise.

Let worry fall.

Prayer

Dear God, quiet my mind and steady my heart. Fill me with Your peace. Amen.

Takeaway

Peace is your reset button.

Pause here.

You've finished Day 2.

"My peace I give you." — John 14:27

Return tomorrow for Day 3.

Day 3 —
Reset Your Strength

Scripture

"Those who hope in the Lord will renew their strength." — Isaiah 40:31

Reflection

You don't need more willpower — you need renewal.

Today is about receiving strength instead of trying to manufacture it.

Heart Moment

You are not weak —

you're being refilled.

Prayer

Dear God, renew my strength today. Lift what feels heavy and energize my spirit. Amen.

Takeaway

Strength returns when you rest in God.

Pause here.

You've finished Day 3.

"Those who hope in the Lord will renew their strength." — Isaiah 40:31

Return tomorrow for Day 4.

Day 4 —
Reset Your Focus

Scripture

"Fix your eyes on Jesus." — *Hebrews 12:2*

Reflection

A scattered mind leads to a scattered life.

Today is about narrowing your focus to what truly matters — God's voice, God's presence, God's direction.

Heart Moment

Not everything deserves your attention.

Choose what aligns with your purpose.

Prayer

Dear God, help me focus on what You're
doing and ignore what distracts me. Amen.

Takeaway

What you focus on shapes your future.

Pause here.

You've finished Day 4.

"Fix your eyes on Jesus." — Hebrews 12:2

Return tomorrow for Day 5.

Day 5 —
Reset Your Heart

Scripture

"Create in me a clean heart, O God."
— *Psalm 51:10*

Reflection

Your heart holds emotions, memories, and wounds.

Today is about letting God cleanse, soften, and heal the places you've been carrying quietly.

Heart Moment

Healing begins when you stop hiding what hurts.

Prayer

Dear God, heal my heart and make it whole again. Amen.

Takeaway

A healed heart sees life differently.

Pause here.

You've finished Day 5.

"Create in me a clean heart, O God."

— Psalm 51:10

Return tomorrow for Day 6.

Day 6 —
Reset Your Identity

Scripture

"You are God's masterpiece."
— *Ephesians 2:10*

Reflection

A reset means remembering who you are — and who you are not.

Today is about shedding old labels and embracing your God-given identity.

Heart Moment

You are not your past.
You are not your mistakes.
You are God's.

Prayer

Dear God, remind me who I am in You.
Silence every lie that says otherwise. Amen.

Takeaway

Identity shapes destiny.

Pause here.

You've finished Day 6.

"You are God's masterpiece."

— Ephesians 2:10

Return tomorrow for Day 7.

Day 7 —
Reset Your Purpose

Scripture

"The Lord will fulfill His purpose for me." — Psalm 138:8

Reflection

A reset ends with direction.

Today is about stepping into the next chapter with clarity, confidence, and renewed purpose.

Heart Moment

You are not starting over — you're starting fresh.

Prayer

Dear God, guide my steps and align my life with Your purpose. Amen.

Takeaway

A reset prepares you for what's next.

Pause here.

End of Day 7.

"The Lord will fulfill His purpose for me." —
Psalm 138:8

Take time today to reflect on the truth and purpose you've discovered.

Let Day 7's message guide your thoughts throughout the day.

Ask God to guide your next steps.

Continue Your Journey

Whenever you're ready, return to Day 1 and let God speak again. Every cycle brings a new layer of clarity, healing, and purpose. As you begin each new cycle, let these Scriptures guide your heart through each day's reset:

- Be transformed by the *renewing* of your mind.
- My *peace* I give you.
- Those who hope in the Lord will renew their *strength*.
- Fix your eyes on *Jesus*.
- Create in me a clean *heart*, O God.
- You are God's *masterpiece*.
- The Lord will fulfill His *purpose* for me.

Each time you walk through these seven days, let God's truth settle deeper in your heart. Trust that God will meet you in new ways and reveal fresh insights each time you return.

If these seven days have awakened a deeper desire to hear God, walk with Him, and live from a place of steady peace, there's a meaningful next step. My book, *The Love of God: Your User Guide to Supernatural Intelligence,* is the foundation behind this devotional. RESET draws from its core truths and practices. If you'd like to go deeper, you can find the book on Amazon— it will help you recognize God's voice, understand His guidance, and build a lasting, intimate connection with Him.

Your walk with God continues—one moment, one whisper at a time. Each step you take draws you closer to the peace, clarity, and purpose you were created for.

A Blessing for the Road Ahead

May God renew your mind, restore your peace, and strengthen your heart as you move forward.

May you notice His presence in the small moments, the ordinary rhythms, and the unexpected places. And when life feels scattered, may you remember you can always return—to stillness, to truth, to Him.

Go forward with grace.

Go forward with purpose.

Go forward with God.

Author's Note

Thank you for walking through these seven days with me.

RESET was born out of my own need to slow down, breathe deeply, and return to God. I wrote these reflections during a season when life felt scattered, and I needed simple, steady truths to anchor me.

My hope is that these pages have met you in your own season—whether you came here weary, searching, hopeful, or simply hungry for more of God.

Every reset is an invitation, gently drawing you back to Him, reminding you that you are loved, seen, and held.

If this devotional has stirred something deeper in you, I pray you continue to follow that pull. God delights in revealing Himself to those who seek Him.

Thank you for letting me be part of your journey.

— D.D. Stumpf

You will seek me and find me when you seek me with all your heart.

— Jeremiah 29:13 (NIV)

About the Author

D.D. Stumpf writes about hearing God and cultivating a personal relationship with Him. Her work helps readers develop a direct, daily connection with God through simple, practical pathways.

She is the author of *The Love of God: Your Guide to Supernatural Intelligence (Create a Direct Connection with God)* and is passionate about helping people experience God's presence with confidence and ease.

If this devotional blessed you, please consider leaving a review on Amazon. Your words help other readers discover RESET and begin their own journey back to God. Thank you for being part of this seven-day reset.

Resources

If you'd like a simple way to stay rooted in Scripture beyond these seven days, the YouVersion Bible App is a beautiful companion. It's free, easy to use, and filled with reading plans that can help you stay connected to God's voice. You can find it here:

https://www.youversion.com/bible-app